MW00889981

Thank you for purchasing our book of
Daily Affirmations and supporting Street
Cat Publishing. We hope reading it brings
you lots of peace, joy and happiness. Please
visit our Amazon store to check out our
other items or to leave a review.

Table of Contents

Introduction

Daily affirmations are positive statements that you repeat to yourself on a regular basis.to help you reflect and bring peace and balance to your life. They can be about anything you want to improve, such as your self-esteem, your relationships, your career, or your health.

There are many different ways to use positive affirmations. You can write them down, say them aloud, or even think them to yourself. Anything that will help you keep them present throughout the day. The most important thing is to be consistent with your practice. The more you repeat an affirmation, the more powerful it will become.

This book contains 365 daily affirmations, one for each day of the year.

When you repeat these positive affirmations to yourself, you are essentially retraining your brain to think more positively. This can lead to a number of benefits, including:

Increased self-esteem
Improved mood
Reduced stress
Increased motivation
Better sleep
Stronger relationships
Improved health

Daily affirmations are a simple but powerful tool that can help you improve your well-being and promote inner peace.

If you are looking for a way to boost your self-esteem, reduce stress, and improve your overall happiness, then I encourage you to give daily affirmations a try.

January 1

I am an unstoppable force of nature.

January 2

Today is an opportunity to grow and learn.

January 3

I am proud of myself and my achievements.

January 4

I believe that I can do anything.

January 5

I am a good person who deserves happiness, health, and peace.

January 6

I am a unique individual with my own unique perspective.

January 7

I am committed to finding inner peace and harmony.

January 8

I am grateful for this life.

January 9

I know that I am not alone and that there are people who can help me.

January 10

I will accomplish everything I need to do today.

January 11

I am not afraid to take risks or challenges.

January 12

I believe that everything that happens in my life is happening for a reason.

January 13

I am confident and believe in myself.

January 14

I have a place at the table.

January 15

I do my best, and my best is good enough.

January 16

I am capable of unconditional love.

January 17

Changing my mind is a strength, not a weakness.

January 18

I am kind and compassionate toward others.

January 19

There is beauty in everything, if I look for it.

January 20

I can choose who I want to spend my time with.

January 21

When I forgive myself, I free myself.

January 22

I prioritize my well-being.

January 23

I make time for activities that bring me joy and relaxation.

January 24

Sometimes the best way to get ahead is to slow down.

January 25
I allow myself to feel my feelings without judgment.

January 26
I have goals and dreams that I am going to achieve.

January 27
When I am connected to my purpose, I am fearless.

January 28
I am aware of my needs and address them accordingly.

January 29

I am grateful for the wealth that I have.

January 30

I am feeling healthy and strong today.

January 31

I am worthy of love and respect.

February 1

I am not afraid to make mistakes, because I know that I can learn from them.

February 2

I won't stop at anything to achieve my goals.

February 3

It is possible to change your mind without being afraid or ashamed.

February 4

I challenge myself to do things that I'm afraid of.

February 5

I am living with abundance.

February 6

When I let go of negativity and stress, I open myself up to new possibilities.

February 7

I allow myself to give and receive love.

February 8

I am not afraid to be myself.

February 9

There are some things I can't change, and I'm okay with that.

February 10

I am kind and compassionate toward myself.

February 11

I am grateful for the many blessings in my life.

February 12

I am not ashamed of my emotions.

February 13

I have what I need to take on the day.

February 14
I am capable of balance in my life.

February 15
I am proud of my ability to make worthwhile contributions to the world.

February 16
I spread joy wherever I go.

February 17
I am respecting my own needs and wants.

February 18

Everything is going to be okay.

February 19

I allow myself to feel good.

February 20

My happiness does not come at the expense of others.

February 21

I love, and I am loved.

February 22

I deserve to be happy.

February 23

I am spreading positivity
and hope.

February 24

I am grateful for my
body and all that it does
for me.

February 25

There is always
something to be grateful
for.

February 26
My ideas are unique and important.

February 27
I am growing one day at a time, one step at a time.

February 28
I am grateful for all the love and support I receive.

March 1
I lift others up, just as I lift myself up.

March 2

I give myself permission to heal.

March 3

I alone am enough.

March 4

Vulnerability is not weakness.

March 5

I am resilient in the face of challenges.

March 6

I am driven by my vision and I am committed to achieving my goals.

March 7

My life is not a race or competition.

March 8

I am making a difference in the world

March 9

I am perfect just the way I am.

March 10

I am surrounded by positive people who believe in me.

March 11

I listen to my inner voice.

March 12

I am proud of myself.

March 13

I am responsible for my own happiness.

March 14

Today I will focus on
what makes me feel good.

March 15

Growth can happen in
quiet moments.

March 16

I am confident in my
ability to succeed.

March 17

I am in harmony and
balanced with my life.

March 18

I am willing to ask for help when I need it.

March 19

I choose myself.

March 20

I am optimistic and always look for the bright side of situations.

March 21

I am worthy of all the good life has to offer..

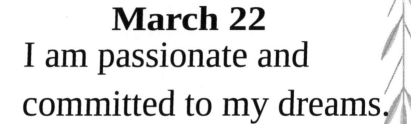

March 22
I am passionate and committed to my dreams.

March 23
My identity is my own and no one else can define it for me.

March 24
I have the right to feel my feelings.

March 25
I am growing stronger and more capable every day.

March 26

I deserve to be treated with kindness.

March 27

I am not being selfish by asking for what I want.

March 28

It's okay to take care of yourself.

March 29

When I accept myself for who I am, I find inner peace.

March 30

I am grateful for the abundance in my life.

March 31

I can find a balance between hard work and relaxation

April 1

I am not giving in to fear or anger.

April 2

I am allowed to feel good.

April 3

I am here to shine my light on the world.

April 4

I am a work of art and I want to celebrate my body.

April 5

I believe in myself.

April 6

I am worthy of what I desire.

April 7

I am no longer limited by my old beliefs.

April 8

I am a healthy and happy person.

April 9

I am grateful for the gift of another day.

April 10

I am focused on my goals.

April 11

I am in charge of my life.

April 12

I am surrounded by love, joy, and abundance.

April 13

I trust my inner compass and follow it.

April 14

I am beautiful, inside and out, no matter what my size.

April 15

I choose to feel peaceful.

April 16

I am open to all the opportunities life brings my way.

April 17

When I am grounded, I am strong.

April 18

I am a strong individual who attracts success and happiness.

April 19

I am open-minded and I am always willing to try new things

April 20

I am not afraid to stand out from the crowd.

April 21

I accept who I am.

April 22

I know each day is a blessing and a gift.

April 23

When you let go of your attachments, you become more open to new experiences.

April 24

I am persistent and don't give up easily.

April 25

I am free to create the life I want.

April 26

I am a positive force in the world.

April 27

I am not afraid to speak my truth

April 28

I belong here.

April 29

I am grateful for the present moment.

April 30

I allow myself to feel my emotions.

May 1

I am a capable and resilient person who is destined for great things.

May 2

There is room in my life for joy and abundance.

May 3

I will embrace change and growth.

May 4

I am not defined by my problems.

May 5

I am centered and I stay calm in the face of adversity.

May 6

I am loved and accepted for who I am.

May 7

I am grateful for another day of life.

May 8

I am constantly striving to improve myself and achieve my goals.

May 9

I am loved and appreciated by those who matter most.

May 10

When I feel lost, I turn to my inner wisdom and guidance.

May 11

My mental health is just as important as my physical health.

May 12

Good things continually happen to me.

May 13

I welcome the wisdom that comes with growing older.

May 14

I take care of myself, mind, body, and spirit.

May 15

I can be anything I want to be.

May 16

I believe in myself.

May 17

I am adventurous and seek out new experiences.

May 18

I am content and free from pain.

May 19

I am grateful for everything I have in my life.

May 20

I am a friend to my body.

May 21

I am open to limitless possibilities.

May 22

I release what no longer serves me.

May 23

I am independent and self-sufficient.

May 24

I am doing the work that works best for me.

May 25

I accept myself for who I am.

May 26

I am honest and authentic.

May 27

I choose to focus on the positive and find joy in the everyday.

May 28

My opinion matters.

May 29

I am proud of who I am
and I let my light shine
through.

May 30

I am able to let go of
tension and worry.

May 31

I am unafraid to ask for
what I need.

June 1

I am good and getting
better.

June 2

I achieve whatever I set my mind to.

June 3

I am honest with myself and others about my needs and desires.

June 4

I can be whatever I want to be.

June 5

My feelings are allowed to be felt.

June 6

I am growing and I am going at my own pace.

June 7

I welcome rest and stillness.

June 8

I am committed to creating healthy and supportive relationships.

June 9

I am making positive choices for myself.

June 10

I am not limited by my past experiences.

June 11

I can accept my feelings without judgment.

June 12

It is enough to do my best.

June 13

I am always looking for the magic in the ordinary.

June 14

I deserve freedom and peace.

June 15

I wake up motivated.

June 16

I am worthy of good things.

June 17

I strive for joy, not for perfection.

June 18

I use challenges to motivate me to learn and grow.

June 19

I choose hope.

June 20

I am brave even when I feel fear.

June 21

Today will be a productive day.

June 22

I am accepted and supported by those who love me.

June 23

I seek beauty in all things.

June 24

I release the fears that do not help me.

June 25

I embrace my uniqueness.

June 26

I am capable of experiencing a wide range of emotions at once.

June 27

I am in charge of how I feel and I choose to feel happy.

June 28

My body knows how to heal itself.

June 29

I am intelligent and focused.

June 30

I am loved and worthy.

July 1

I can do anything

July 2

I am following my heart.

July 3

Positivity is a choice that
I choose to make.

July 4

I practice gratitude for all that I have, and all that is yet to come.

July 5

I am taking in strength and releasing weakness.

July 6

All the love I need is within me right now.

July 7

I will be open to different perspectives and experiences.

July 8

I nourish myself with loving words and healthy foods.

July 9

I am safe and grounded in my life..

July 10

I feel more grateful each day.

July 11

I am accepting myself unconditionally.

July 12

I allow myself to feel my emotions, even the difficult ones.

July 13

I am a force for good in the world.

July 14

I trust myself to make the right decisions.

July 15

I only compare myself to myself.

July 16

I have the power to make a difference in someone's life.

July 17

I am more than my circumstances dictate.

July 18

I am getting healthier every day.

July 19

I listen to my inner voice and follow my gut feeling.

July 20

I joyfully learn more about what I don't know.

July 21

My commitment to myself is real.

July 22

I am open to healing.

July 23

Each and every day, I am getting closer to achieving my goals.

July 24

I have endless strength.

July 25

I am a source of inspiration and encouragement.

July 26

I am optimistic because today is a new day.

July 27

I am constantly learning, changing, and growing.

July 28

I am inspired by the
things that I love.

July 29

I can do hard things.

July 30

I look forward to
tomorrow and the
opportunities that await
me.

July 31

I am kind and
compassionate towards
all people.

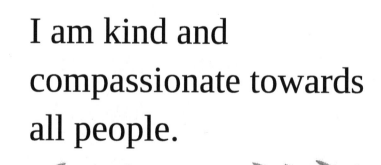

August 1

Incredible changes are happening in me right now.

August 2

I am so much stronger than I realize.

August 3

I am a winner.

August 4

I am peaceful and whole.

August 5

I am constantly growing and evolving into a better person.

August 6

I accept that some things are not meant for me.

August 7

I am important and my voice matters.

August 8

I am a positive force for good in the world.

August 9

I am worthy of love,
respect, and happiness.

August 10

I am getting better and
better every day.

August 11

I have the power to face
any difficulty.

August 12

I'm freeing myself from
all destructive fear and
doubts.

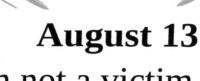

August 13

I am not a victim of my circumstances.

August 14

Even in hard times, I trust that everything will be okay.

August 15

I am willing to embrace the unexpected.

August 16

I am worthy of love and acceptance, just as I am.

August 17

I am not defined by the words that others say about me.

August 18

Everything will work out for me.

August 19

I am safe and surrounded by love and support.

August 20

I am unique and special, and I embrace my differences.

August 21

I am powerful.

August 22

I am doing what I am meant to do.

August 23

I am accepting myself for who I am, flaws and all.

August 24

I am still learning so it's okay to make mistakes.

August 25

I use my voice to speak
up for myself and others.

August 26

I am open to new ways
of improving my health.

August 27

It will all be okay.

August 28

I am confident in my
ability to create positive
change.

August 29
I am healing and getting stronger every day.

August 30
I am understood and my ideas are important.

August 31
Today is a new opportunity to make a positive impact.

September 1
I trust that I'm heading in the right direction.

September 2

I have what I need to take on the day.

September 3

Everything is easy for me to handle.

September 4

I am valued and helpful.

September 5

I am able to find calm and serenity in the midst of chaos.

September 6

I am enough. I have enough.

September 7

I invite abundance and a generous heart.

September 8

I know there is good in every situation.

September 9

I am confident in the presence of others.

September 10

My happiness is contagious.

September 11

I allow myself to make mistakes as they help me grow.

September 12

I am well-rested and ready for the day.

September 13

I am going to come out stronger on the other side.

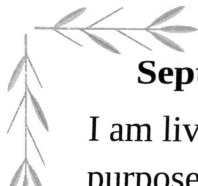

September 14

I am living my life with purpose and intention.

September 15

I embrace all the possibilities today brings.

September 16

I am not afraid to think outside the box.

September 17

I am worthy of happiness.

September 18

I accept myself exactly
as I am without judgment.

September 19

I am filled with hope and
optimism.

September 20

I am capable of giving
and receiving love.

September 21

I do not waste a single
day of my life.

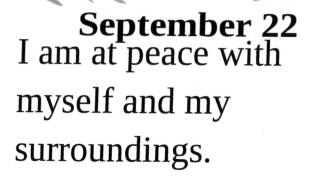

September 22

I am at peace with myself and my surroundings.

September 23

I belong here, and I deserve to take up space.

September 24

Happiness is a choice, and today I choose to be happy.

September 25

I have everything I need to achieve my goals.

September 26

Happiness is within my reach.

September 27

I am at peace with myself and my life.

September 28

I put my energy into things that matter to me.

September 29

I am filled with gratitude and surrounded by love.

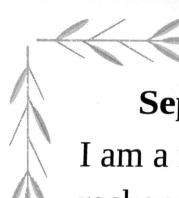

September 30

I am a force to be
reckoned with.

October 1

With every breath, I feel
stronger.

October 2

I am confident in my
decisions.

October 3

I deserve to be kind to
myself.

October 4
I am always open to learning something new.

October 5
I am able to make sound judgments and decisions.

October 6
I walk away when a person or a situation isn't healthy for me.

October 7
I am confident in my ability to come up with brilliant ideas.

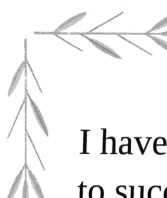

October 8

I have everything I need to succeed.

October 9

I have nothing to prove.

October 10

I go through life one step at a time.

October 11

I can be gentle and nurturing, but I can also be assertive and strong.

October 12

I am prepared for anything today brings.

October 13

I am safe and supported.

October 14

I belong in this world; there are people that care about me.

October 15

I can control how I respond to things that are out of my control.

October 16

I trust myself to make the right decision.

October 17

I am in control of my thoughts.

October 18

My past might be ugly, but I am still beautiful.

October 19

My ideas and perspectives are valuable.

October 20

I love and accept myself.

October 21

I make the world a better place.

October 22

I am a source of light and love.

October 23

I am building my own path.

October 24

I am overjoyed to live this amazing life.

October 25

I am not afraid to feel my emotions.

October 26

I have made mistakes, but I will not let them define me.

October 27

I am becoming more present and aware.

October 28

Everything is fine.

October 29

I am ready for all the amazing things this day has in store for me.

October 30

I have come farther than I would have ever thought possible.

October 31

I am always headed in the right direction.

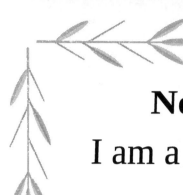

November 1

I am a shining light.

November 2

I am coming closer to my true self every day.

November 3

I am driven and determined.

November 4

I don't compare myself to others.

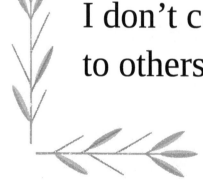

November 5

My voice matters.

November 6

Every day, I am growing.

November 7

I am kind to myself and others.

November 8

I contain unlimited amounts of ambition and strength.

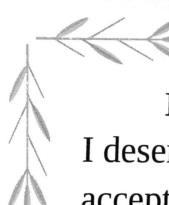

November 9
I deserve to be loved and accepted for who I am.

November 10
I embrace challenges as opportunities for growth.

November 11
I am worthy of good health.

November 12
I am grateful for the abundance in my life.

November 13

I'm meeting my own definition of success.

November 14

I trust that I am on the right path.

November 15

My passion fuels my progress.

November 16

I deserve to take time for myself.

November 17

I am in control of my future.

November 18

I am grateful to have people in my life who care for me.

November 19

I deserve self-respect and love.

November 20

I choose to think positively.

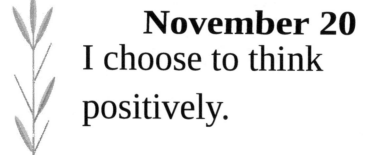

November 21

I am fearless in the face of obstacles.

November 22

I reach towards my goals, like a flower growing towards the sun.

November 23

I am a willing participant in my own well being.

November 24

I believe in my ability to make a difference.

November 25

I finish what matters and let go of what does not.

November 26

My happiness is up to me.

November 27

I am resilient and bounce back from adversity.

November 28

I do all things in love.

November 29

I can take deep breaths.

November 30

I am focused on the journey, not just the destination.

December 1

I nourish my soul with positive thoughts, feelings, and experiences.

December 2

I am inspired by the world around me.

December 3

I am willing to work
hard to achieve my goals.

December 4

I have the power to
change my life.

December 5

I am letting go of stress
and anxiety.

December 6

My life has meaning.
What I do is important.

December 7

I am learning valuable lessons from myself every day.

December 8

I am confident in my decisions.

December 9

I am not afraid to ask questions.

December 10

I trust my intuition.

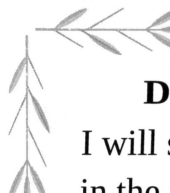

December 11

I will stay positive even in the face of negativity.

December 12

I am allowed to take breaks.

December 13

I do not pretend to be anyone or anything other than who I am.

December 14

My positive attitude attracts happy people.

December 15

I am at peace with who I am as a person.

December 16

I celebrate my achievements.

December 17

I am persistent.

December 18

I am not dependent on another person for my happiness.

December 19

I will embrace change and growth.

December 20

I am grateful for all the opportunities that come my way.

December 21

Anything is possible.

December 22

I have the courage to take risks.

December 23

I am my own champion.

December 24

I am the author of my
own story.

December 25

I am proud of the things I
accomplished today.

December 26

I radiate positive energy.

December 27

Rest is required to achieve growth.

December 28

My life does not have to be perfect to be happy.

December 29

Wonderful things are going to happen to me.

December 30

I set goals and go after them with all the determination I have.

December 31

I embrace change and rise to the new opportunity it brings.

I hope this book has bought you much love, peace and happiness throughout the year.

Made in the USA
Las Vegas, NV
30 November 2024

aca39e40-363f-4aae-8004-75d117d1a1e5R01